THE TEACHER'S REFLECTIVE CALENDAR AND PLANNING JOURNAL

To all teachers who have given their best to make a positive difference in the lives of the children they serve every day.

THE TEACHER'S REFLECTIVE CALENDAR AND PLANNING JOURNAL

Motivation, Inspiration, and Affirmation

Mary Zabolio McGrath • Beverley Holden Johns

CORWIN PRESS
A SAGE Publications Company
Thousand Oaks, California

For information:

Corwin Press
A Sage Publications Company
2455 Teller Road
Thousand Oaks, California 91320
www.corwinpress.com

Sage Publications Ltd.
1 Oliver's Yard
55 City Road
London EC1Y 1SP
United Kingdom

Sage Publications India Pvt. Ltd.
B-42, Panchsheel Enclave
Post Box 4109
New Delhi 110 017 India

Printed in the United States of America

ISBN 978-1-4129-2645-4 (cloth)
ISBN 978-1-4129-2646-1 (pbk.)

This book is printed on acid-free paper.

07   08   09   10   9   8   7   6   5   4   3   2

Acquisitions Editor:	Faye Zucker
Editorial Assistant:	Gem Rabanera
Production Editor:	Beth A. Bernstein
Copy Editor:	Diana Breti
Typesetter:	C&M Digitals (P) Ltd.
Proofreader:	Libby Larson
Cover Designer:	Rose Storey

Contents

Preface

What can I do to improve my relationship with the parents of my students? How can I organize my classroom better so that I can find items quickly? How do I prepare my students for standardized tests? These are questions that you may ask yourself daily. Each of us is continually searching for new ideas to improve our teaching skills. Professional growth as a teacher is an ongoing process. There is always something new to learn.

Together, we have over 70 years of experience in education. We have designed this calendar journal to incorporate our experience and perspectives and to provide practical advice. We not only want to share our ideas; we want to provide you with the tools to set goals and to reflect upon your daily teaching experiences.

This daily planner/journal will motivate and support you through journaling and goal setting. In this day and age, teachers maintain busy schedules and keep closely connected to their calendars. By including a reflective component in a teacher planner, we invite you to consider your daily successes and challenges and to focus on goals to improve day by day.

In this planner, there is a space for every day of the year. One idea or inspirational thought is presented for each day, and space is provided for you to write down your thoughts and goals. Extra space is offered for more goal setting as well. You are invited to write about the high points of your teaching day and events that may inspire a change or new direction for the next day. We offer you a design and a process. We encourage you to view the events of your school day as they unfold. In so doing, we challenge you to not only fully involve yourself in each day's events, but also to look for occurrences that call for reflection, events that challenge you to redirect your teaching strategies, and dynamics in your day that give you inspiration.

We encourage you to step back at the end of each school day and notice not only the apparent and obvious events that have stuck in your mind, but also other things. While taking time to reflect, you will be giving yourself the space and opportunity to focus on the less obvious occurrences and to recall the impressions that you had but have not had time to really examine. For example, during the time routinely set aside for reflection, you will be giving yourself the chance to review nuances, subtleties, and signals that were not noticed immediately. When you go back over the day, such messages come to you because by taking this specified time you invite them to come forth. Perhaps a child's wordless messages in the form of a facial expression will speak volumes when considered in the context of other events. Maybe an offhand comment made by a colleague will lead you to a realization that would never have surfaced in your busy day, yet results in a decision and direction important for you professionally. Something you see, hear, or "feel in your gut" may move to center stage during the quiet time that you routinely set aside for yourself. With this planner before you, your heart, mind, and personal insights and perceptions can aid you in finding your way, not only in your teaching but also in your relationships with students, parents, and staff.

This calendar journal is full of our best ideas to make your teaching more rewarding and to provide you with a daily system of support in your work. We want to encourage you to stay in the profession, and perhaps this calendar will be the bright and sunny pick-me-up to get you off to a good start each day. Not only does this calendar have a new idea each day based on a monthly topic, but it also provides spaces for goals and your "to do" list. We encourage you to take a few minutes at the end of each day for yourself and to reflect on the best thing that happened to you that day and your thoughts about the day's occurrences. We further suggest that you use the results of your reflection to influence your work for the next day.

Our hope is that this calendar will outline a path that is both broad and deep. As you begin to work the process each day, may you grow in the ability to access your best insights—insights that would have been lost if you hadn't given yourself the time to stop and reflect about your day. In so doing, may your ideas lead to further creative, unique, and effective offerings for your students. By listening to the teaching talent within you and processing your day, you are going deep within yourself to find the fullness of your teaching ability in order to present to your students ideas that will have a broad impact on them now and in the future.

This calendar offers you a new idea daily to improve your professional career—366 ideas are provided to assist you in your professional and personal life. Each month has a specific focus. For example, September focuses on getting to know your students, January focuses on preparing students for testing, and March focuses on maintaining motivation. We have focused on topics we believe teachers will find workable and helpful. You can adapt these ideas to meet your own needs in the classroom. The ideas are designed for a wide variety of grade levels. You may not want to use the exact idea but may want to utilize some variation of it. Perhaps one of our ideas will trigger many other similar ideas that you can utilize in your classroom and your life. There is an air of excitement for all of us when we get a new idea and try it in our classroom. We hope these ideas will motivate and inspire you to meet your goals.

We recognize that your goals do not remain within the confines of your classroom or even your school. As a whole person, you bring your fullest self into the process of teaching. While working with students, you may be thinking of picking up a prescription on the way home or exercising at the health club on the way to school. Items such as these can be placed on this daily schedule as well. Perhaps at the end of a difficult day, when you sit with the calendar, you may decide that you need to break a potential cycle of stress and commit to an early bike ride before getting ready for the next school day. Recognizing your personal needs in response to the school day helps make the school day more manageable.

When summer comes, you will still have the opportunity to see your personal life and your career life as a whole. This is part of the same concept. Ideas gained from taking a summer graduate class can be recorded in the calendar and easily accessed once you are teaching again. Perhaps while weeding the garden in July you will think of an idea to supplement a unit that you teach in January. Having this calendar available will help you remember to incorporate the idea when school is again in full swing.

When planning the upcoming day, it is critical that we contemplate what we want to accomplish that day—accomplishments that will make a difference in the success of our day as a teacher. Written goal setting is a skill that we want to teach our students, regardless of their ages. It gives them something to work toward. And then, at the end of the day, what a great experience it is for them to look back and see that their goals were achieved. We teachers must also set goals for ourselves. Writing down those goals makes it more likely that we will work to achieve them. The calendar includes a place where you can write down your goals. Daily goals may be added in the reflection spaces as well. We owe it to ourselves to begin our day with a goal in mind; we all need something to work toward. One goal might be to increase the use of praise with a specific student, or another might be to incorporate a mnemonic device into a social studies lesson. On Saturday or Sunday, a goal might be to read a chapter of an educational or inspirational book. There may be times that we are tempted to write that our goal is to just survive the day, but we need to resist this temptation and think of something meaningful to accomplish during each day—*what will make a difference in the life of a student?* Goals keep us focused, and when we have met our goals, we feel a tremendous sense of accomplishment.

You also have a place to make a to-do list. We always have a sense of completion when we can cross off items during our day. Making a list also enables us to evaluate how much we are trying to take on. If the list is too long, are there items that can be deleted or moved to a future date? However we choose to use a to-do list, it is a means to gain a sense of mastery over our work days.

When a year is completed and we have reviewed our days, a completed calendar can be used as a reference for the future. In fact, following one school year with another reflective calendar reinforces the process you have begun. Having two copies of the month of March for comparison, for example, provides a record of how far your students have come in mastering certain concepts, your mood and energy level during this time of year, and even your plans for spring break renewal. Keeping a log of your professional life and its connection to your personal self, both your inner thoughts and feelings and the external events you experience, gives a sense of the fullness of your life. The calendar, both as a journal of your private reflections and a record of the events in your classroom and your professional growth, can become more valuable to you with use, application, and the collection of content.

Finally, we all have learned from our experiences—our successes and our failures. At the end of the day, we need to stop and reflect on the happenings of the day. This process causes us to take some time for ourselves, to pause and reflect, and to write down our thoughts. You may think that you don't have time, but remember, you owe it to yourself to take five or ten minutes to think about the successes and challenges that you faced. You may think that nothing has gone well during the day, but when you sit down to reflect and think about the good things that happened or an excellent lesson you taught, you feel better and feel that the day was a success in many ways. What a great way to end the day—on a positive note. At the end of the week or the month or the year, you will find it most helpful to review various days and see your reflections and what you learned throughout the year. Your legacy of experience will not only be beneficial to you but also to other teachers. What a rewarding experience to keep a journal and review it five years later and look at what happened during that time. You can see the professional growth that you have experienced—and have the opportunity to reminisce about years past.

To take the time to review our yesterdays, to reflect on today, and determine our tomorrows is a gift we can give ourselves that enriches our lives. When we see the events of life, both personal and professional, we realize that we are aware and connected to our world. We gain perspective from seeing the regularity of the positive gifts in life. We gain confidence and courage when we realize that we have managed stressful challenges with educated and mature choices and the application of our training.

We may feel stress in our everyday work, and writing down our thoughts is a great stress reducer. It assists us to compile our thoughts and to realize that maybe something that was upsetting during the day wasn't really that big an issue. We may also be able to gain more insight into certain events when we write them down.

Because a teacher's day is intense and busy, you may not always find the time to process the occurrences of a day that had significant impact on you. Sometimes it is by mentioning moments to others that we come to realize what really mattered in any given day. Yet because teachers get so busy and have so many demands placed on them, it can be difficult to really address the issues that truly mean something. We do not always have that ideal companion with us. But by using the reflective process in the following pages, you can reinforce your relationship with yourself and make this calendar a helpful professional and personal companion.

Those of us in the field of education must support ourselves—by journaling, taking time to learn from the experiences of others, and setting goals. Reflection will assist us to be the best educator we can be. We must also support each other—by sharing our wealth of experiences with those who succeed us. This calendar has been designed as that support tool. Read on for the wealth of ideas that are available to you—our offerings and legacy to you. Consider each day an opportunity to grow as a professional. We wish you a wonderful year full of successes in the classroom and in your life.

ACKNOWLEDGMENTS

Corwin Press gratefully acknowledges the contributions of the following reviewers:

Mary Gale Budzisz
Retired Special Education Teacher
Pawleys Island, SC

Mary Camp
Special Services Coordinator
Peoria Public Schools
Peoria, IL

Thomas S.C. Farrell
Associate Professor
Brock University
Ontario, Canada

Laura M. Frey
Assistant Professor
Central Michigan University
Mount Pleasant, MI

Jennifer York-Barr
Associate Professor
University of Minnesota
Minneapolis, MN

About the Authors

Mary Zabolio McGrath taught with the Bloomington Minnesota Public Schools for 31 years. This included teaching Grade 3, Project Read, and special education in the areas of learning disabilities, behavioral disorders, and developmental delay.

In addition, Mary is a professional speaker and writer. She authored *Teachers Today: A Guide to Surviving Creatively, Teachers in Transition: Growing Forward Through Retirement,* and *Surviving Internal Politics Within the School: Practical Strategies for Teachers,* with Beverley Johns and Sarup Mathur. She offers workshops to teachers, parents, and organizations based on the themes and concepts in her books. Mary belongs to the National Speakers Association and Toastmasters International.

Mary has served as national secretary for the Council for Behavior Disorders and held the position of state treasurer and secretary for that organization. She is the recipient of both the Frank Wood Award and the Sheldon Braaten Award given by the Minnesota Council for Children with Behavioral Disorders. Currently, she serves on the board for the Minnesota Council for Exceptional Children.

Beverley Holden Johns has 35 years' experience working with students with learning disabilities and students with severe behavioral disorders within the public schools of Illinois. She supervised learning disabilities teachers in 22 school districts and was the founder and administrator of the Garrison Alternative School for students with severe behavioral disorders in Jacksonville, Illinois, and later the coordinator for staff development for the Four Rivers Special Education District. She is now a learning and behavior consultant and also an adjunct instructor for MacMurray College.

She will chair the 10th Biennial Conference of the International Association of Special Education (IASE) in Hong Kong (2007) and serve as president of IASE (2008–2009). She presented the Inaugural Marden Lecture at the University of Hong Kong in January 2006.

Beverley is the lead author of eight books (and coauthor of one other) including *Reduction of School Violence: Alternatives to Suspension*; *Techniques for Managing Verbally and Physically Aggressive Students*; *Surviving Internal Politics Within the School: Practical Strategies for Teachers*; *Safe Schools*; *The Teacher's Reflective Calendar and Planning Journal*; *Effective Curriculum and Instruction for Students With Emotional/ Behavioral Disorders*; *Students With Disabilities and General Education: A Desktop Reference for School Personnel*; *Getting Behavioral Interventions Right*; and *Preparing Test-Resistant Students for Assessments: A Staff Training Guide*. She has written a workbook to accompany a video for paraprofessionals entitled: *The Paraprofessional's Guide to Managing Student Behavior*. She is lead author of a monograph on successful inclusion of E/BD students and an article on leadership in special education (in addition to over 40 others).

She is the 2000 recipient of the CEC Outstanding Leadership Award from the International Council for Exceptional Children, and past international president (and current board member) of the Council for Children with Behavioral Disorders.

Beverley is listed in *Who's Who in America*, *Who's Who of American Women*, *Who's Who in American Education* and *Who's Who Among America's Teachers*. She has served as chair of governmental relations for several national and state organizations concerned with the needs of both regular and general educators and exceptional children. She has chaired ISELA, the Illinois Special Education Coalition, whose membership includes 13 statewide organizations, for 26 years.

She is a past president of the Learning Disabilities Association of Illinois and has been the national state presidents' representative serving on the board of LDA of America.

She was Jacksonville Woman of the Year in 1988, cochaired the Business Education Partnership Committee and the Jacksonville Truancy Task Force.

She has presented workshops across the United States and Canada; San Juan, Puerto Rico; Sydney, Australia (keynote); and Warsaw, Poland.

Beverley is a graduate of Catherine Spalding College in Louisville, Kentucky, and received a fellowship for her graduate work at Southern Illinois University in Carbondale where she received an M.S. in special education. She has done postgraduate work at the University of Illinois, Western Illinois University, SIU, and Eastern Illinois University.

THE TEACHER'S REFLECTIVE CALENDAR AND PLANNING JOURNAL

REALIZING YOUR PURPOSE AND COMMITMENT TO EDUCATION

Date: _____

School is fast approaching, so make an effort to do everything you planned to do this summer. Then direct your thoughts to what you like best about being a teacher.

_____

_____

_____

Date: _____

Gear up for school by stopping into a teacher store or office supply store. Buy something for yourself that will perk up your work area or classroom.

_____

_____

_____

Date: _____

Recognize your feelings about transitioning back to a more structured way of life. What do you feel excited about? What will you miss?

_____

_____

_____

Date: _____

Plan something refreshing and fun for a September weekend. Let the anticipation of this experience motivate you to put your best efforts into setting the tone for the school year during the days ahead.

_____

_____

_____

Date: _____

Take some quiet time to recall when you first thought about being a teacher. Jot down ideas and feelings that surface. Review them often in the next few weeks.

_____

_____

_____

Date: _____

Start imagining creative ways to perk up your classroom routines. For example, have the students pick up scrap paper from the floor to an energetic march, and set out a bright basket for handing in work.

_____

_____

_____

Date: _____

Contact some coworkers and have a frank discussion about any ambivalence felt about returning to school. Ask them why they chose teaching and be open to inspiration.

_____

_____

_____

Things to Do   *Goals*

_____ _____   _____ _____

_____ _____   _____ _____

_____ _____   _____ _____

_____ _____   _____ _____

_____ _____   _____ _____

_____ _____   _____ _____

REALIZING YOUR PURPOSE AND COMMITMENT TO EDUCATION

Date: _____

Do you consider teaching a personal calling? Did you arrive at the decision gradually and gently or like a thunderbolt? Review why you decided to become a teacher.

_____

_____

_____

Date: _____

Consider your contribution to the lives of students and families. Recognize the value that you bring to your school. Take pride in the gifts you give to this profession.

_____

_____

_____

Date: _____

Reconnect with the larger issues and concerns facing education. Consider your potential as one source of the solutions that will positively impact the broader issues.

_____

_____

_____

Date: _____

Commend yourself for already teaching the number of years you have, and resolve to go forward with energy and excellence into the school year ahead.

_____

_____

_____

Date: _____

Visit a school supply store. Watch parents and imagine their hope for their child's future. Consider the student's anticipation and anxiety in facing the unknowns of a new school year.

_____

_____

_____

Date: _____

Read an inspirational book about education. Open yourself to the message presented in the book.

_____

_____

_____

Date: _____

Rent a drama portraying a teacher who helps students in a unique and courageous way. Take to heart the movie's message and consider its application to your upcoming assignment.

_____

_____

_____

Things to Do   *Goals*

_____	_____	_____	_____
_____	_____	_____	_____
_____	_____	_____	_____
_____	_____	_____	_____
_____	_____	_____	_____
_____	_____	_____	_____

REALIZING YOUR PURPOSE AND COMMITMENT TO EDUCATION

Date: _____

Create a timeline of your teaching journey. Include peaks and valleys, naming those who inspired, challenged, and even discouraged you. Add significant experiences and events, both positive and negative.

_____

_____

_____

Date: _____

Whether you start the school year early or wait until the designated day and "hit the ground running," commend yourself for taking your job seriously and preparing wisely.

_____

_____

_____

Date: _____

Search your heart for a piece of wisdom to share with your students. Make it your upcoming annual theme. Imagine ways to reinforce that theme throughout the year.

_____

_____

_____

Date: _____

Remember that the highs and lows, the delights and pressures of this preparation period are the typical elements that catapult you and your colleagues into your next dynamic educational experience.

_____

_____

_____

Date: _____

Recall your first day with a new class. What were the best parts of that day? How can you draw those special highlights into the upcoming first day of school?

_____

_____

_____

Date: _____

Ponder ways to influence the futures of the students in your class this year. Imagine the impact that you will have on each young life placed in your care.

_____

_____

_____

Date: _____

Invent a slogan to keep you going during the next few weeks. Repeat it to yourself often.

_____

_____

_____

Things to Do   *Goals*

_____   _____   _____   _____

_____   _____   _____   _____

_____   _____   _____   _____

_____   _____   _____   _____

_____   _____   _____   _____

REALIZING YOUR PURPOSE AND COMMITMENT TO EDUCATION

Date: _____

Remember your favorite teacher. Why did you appreciate and value this person? How do you imitate this person consciously or unconsciously?

_____

_____

_____

Date: _____

Buy yourself a new outfit or accessory to wear to school. Do you prefer casual comfort, the professional look, or a funny necktie or jewelry to catch your students' attention?

_____

_____

_____

Date: _____

Consider ways to contribute to your community while retaining your identity as a teacher. Realize that you are a valued citizen deserving of respect for your talents and training.

_____

_____

_____

Date: _____

Gain empowerment through recognition that you are part of an immense group of teachers now preparing to return to school.

_____

_____

_____

Date: _____

If you were paid a professional athlete's salary, would that affect the fulfillment you derive from teaching? Focus on events in the days ahead that bring you joy and satisfaction.

_____

_____

_____

Date: _____

Imagine yourself at the preteaching level getting in touch with your hopes and desires for growth. Apply this to your new teaching assignment as a more experienced educator.

_____

_____

_____

Date: _____

Pretend that the school year ahead is your last year as a teacher. How would it be different? What aspects of the job would you especially savor?

_____

_____

_____

Things to Do   *Goals*

_____ _____   _____ _____

_____ _____   _____ _____

_____ _____   _____ _____

_____ _____   _____ _____

_____ _____   _____ _____

_____ _____   _____ _____

REALIZING YOUR PURPOSE AND COMMITMENT TO EDUCATION

Date: _____

Reclaim your unique management and leadership skills that influence coworkers. Resolve to put them to constructive use in the days ahead.

_____

_____

_____

Date: _____

Know that the love in your heart distinguishes you as a teaching professional. Let it flow and give encouragement and affirmation to your students, their families, and colleagues.

_____

_____

_____

Date: _____

Be open to daily inspiration that will help you in each situation you will face. Enjoy the process as creative ideas flow for the benefit of your students and staff.

_____

_____

_____

Date: _____ ^New month!

Write a letter to each child in your classroom before school starts. Invite the child and his or her parents to visit you in your classroom before the first day of school.

_____

_____

_____

GETTING TO KNOW YOUR STUDENTS

Date: _____

Invite your students and their parents to meet you at a neutral site, such as a park or a restaurant. This works wonders in establishing rapport.

_____

_____

_____

Date: _____

Use a personal notebook or e-mail system to engage your students in "dialogue journaling." For each entry a student writes, you write a personal response.

_____

_____

_____

Date: _____

For each student, write a silly secret about yourself. Place the secrets in a basket and each day invite a student to select one to read aloud to the class. Encourage the students to share silly things about themselves as well.

_____

_____

_____

Things to Do   *Goals*

_____ _____   _____ _____

_____ _____   _____ _____

_____ _____   _____ _____

_____ _____   _____ _____

_____ _____   _____ _____

_____ _____   _____ _____

September

GETTING TO KNOW YOUR STUDENTS

Date: _____

Play "This or That." Select two objects and label one "This" and the other "That." Let the students indicate their preferences by standing next to the object that they like best.

_____

_____

_____

Date: _____

Review each student's records from previous school years. Look for strengths and interests. Focus discussions with previous teachers on the positive attributes of the student.

_____

_____

_____

Date: _____

Hang six sheets of chart paper on the walls. Write a prompt at the top of each chart, such as "My biggest pet peeve is." Have each student write his or her name and response on the chart paper.

_____

_____

_____

Date: _____

Establish "lunch with the teacher" for your students on a rotating basis.

_____

_____

_____

Date: _____

 Home visits tell you a great deal about your students. Arrange a home visit with each student, and, if possible, ask an administrator to go with you.

_____

_____

_____

Date: _____

 Hold class meetings. Schedule a time daily or weekly to solve issues that occur in the class.

_____

_____

_____

Date: _____

 Develop and conduct a student interest survey. Include several questions (e.g., What is your favorite TV show? What is your favorite game?).

_____

_____

_____

Things to Do   *Goals*

_____ _____ _____ _____

_____ _____ _____ _____

_____ _____ _____ _____

_____ _____ _____ _____

_____ _____ _____ _____

_____ _____ _____ _____

September

GETTING TO KNOW YOUR STUDENTS

Date: _____

Put a selection of different types of candy into a bowl. Allow each student to select a piece of candy and describe ways that they are similar to it.

_____

_____

_____

Date: _____

Play "Bingo." Have the winner of each game share something about himself or herself.

_____

_____

_____

Date: _____

Ask students to bring in an object that represents them. Have them keep the object secret. Keep it in a secret place so no one identifies the owner. Display all of the objects together, and have the whole class guess the owner of each one.

_____

_____

_____

Date: _____

Create a mnemonic for each student's name. Teach your students about mnemonic devices and how they can be used to remember information.

_____

_____

_____

Date: _____

Give each student an index card. Have the student number the card from 1 to 10. Post a list of numbered questions, and have the students write their answers to the questions on their cards. Have pairs of students exchange cards and introduce each other to the class.

_____

_____

_____

Date: _____

Play "It's in the Bag." Have each student collect things in a bag that depict his or her interests or culture. Let the student display and discuss each item in the collection.

_____

_____

_____

Date: _____

Cut strips of paper and write one question on each strip (e.g., What is your favorite memory?). Place all the strips in a jar. Have one student at a time draw a question, read it aloud, and answer it in front of the class.

_____

_____

_____

Things to Do   *Goals*

_____ _____   _____ _____

_____ _____   _____ _____

_____ _____   _____ _____

_____ _____   _____ _____

_____ _____   _____ _____

_____ _____   _____ _____

September

GETTING TO KNOW YOUR STUDENTS

Date: _____

Write a story starter on the board each day. Have the students complete the story in a journal. Example: I remember the day I

_____

_____

_____

Date: _____

Have each student draw a picture of an apple tree. Have the student write his or her name on the tree trunk and write a personal strength on each apple.

_____

_____

_____

Date: _____

Remember to use good communication skills with students. Speak clearly, use a pleasant tone of voice, and look them in the eye.

_____

_____

_____

Date: _____

Take time to ask the students what they like to do on weekends and after school.

_____

_____

_____

Date: _____

   Show interest in your students' family members. Ask about visits to relatives and friends.

_____

_____

_____

Date: _____

   Students love to talk about their pets. Ask not only whether they have a pet but also when, where, and why they got it.

_____

_____

_____

Date: _____

   Ask each student to name his or her favorite color and to describe why it is his or her favorite.

_____

_____

_____

Things to Do   *Goals*

September

GETTING TO KNOW YOUR STUDENTS

Date: _____

Give each student a note of appreciation to take home to share with his or her family.

_____

_____

_____

Date: _____

Show recognition and give honest praise whenever you can.

_____

_____

_____

Date: _____

Try to find the quality that makes each student special and unique. Give them feedback about that aspect of themselves.

_____

_____

_____

Date: _____

Offer your students a reason to laugh today, whether it is a funny story or a surefire joke.

_____

_____

_____

September – October

ESTABLISHING POSITIVE WORKING RELATIONSHIPS WITH OTHER STAFF MEMBERS

Date: _____

Thank your students whenever they demonstrate good manners to you or to one another.

_____

_____

_____

Date: _____   New month!

Take the time to get to know some basic information about your coworkers. What do they like to do on weekends? Who are their favorite writers? Where do they like to eat?

_____

_____

_____

Date: _____

Join in on topics that interest coworkers. Discuss the weekend game on Monday morning. Ask about their families. Small talk that's meaningful to others goes a long way.

_____

_____

_____

Things to Do   *Goals*

Establishing Positive Working Relationships With Other Staff Members

Date: _____

Spend time in the work spaces of other teachers. Comment on personal photos or objects on their desks.

_____

_____

_____

Date: _____

Notice the efforts of other teachers who have created an interesting bulletin board or a quiet space for students who need downtime.

_____

_____

_____

Date: _____

Offer to assist on committees and projects according to your availability and unique talents.

_____

_____

_____

Date: _____

Invite another staff person for coffee to discuss a team project or simply to relax after work.

_____

_____

_____

Date: _____

Compliment another staff member about help he or she has given to a student that you both work with. For example, recognize the special educator's individualized goals for one of your students. Tell the music teacher how learning to play the violin has increased a student's confidence.

_____

_____

_____

Date: _____

Smile at one person today. Your friendly presence may give him or her the boost he or she needs to make a tough parent call or present a challenging lesson.

_____

_____

_____

Date: _____

Build alliances with those who have a similar school vision to yours. Take time to identify specifics and strategize ways to bring about a plan to better your school climate.

_____

_____

_____

Things to Do   *Goals*

_____ _____   _____ _____

_____ _____   _____ _____

_____ _____   _____ _____

_____ _____   _____ _____

_____ _____   _____ _____

_____ _____   _____ _____

Establishing Positive Working Relationships With Other Staff Members

Date: _____

Recognize the different points of view of your coworkers. How do different people see your school? Their students? What might be their goals and major concerns?

_____

_____

_____

Date: _____

Take time to bring humor into a lunchtime discussion today. Plan what to say to add a light touch when things get too intense or serious.

_____

_____

_____

Date: _____

Find a minute to acknowledge the challenge that office staff face with continuous calls and staff demands. Give them a word of encouragement about their efforts.

_____

_____

_____

Date: _____

Tell custodial staff something you noticed about their reliable upkeep of classrooms, school grounds, or halls.

_____

_____

_____

Date: _____

Stop to welcome a substitute teacher. Offer any current information that may be helpful. Suggest a classroom management strategy that works well with the regular teacher.

_____

_____

_____

Date: _____

Ask your administrator what his or her greatest wish is for the school. Encourage efforts to achieve it and offer your help where appropriate.

_____

_____

_____

Date: _____

When you hear a negative conversation, do your best to avoid joining in. Support anyone being criticized by ignoring comments made about them. Gently bring in a positive perspective on this person.

_____

_____

_____

Things to Do   *Goals*

_____   _____   _____   _____

_____   _____   _____   _____

_____   _____   _____   _____

_____   _____   _____   _____

_____   _____   _____   _____

_____   _____   _____   _____

October

Establishing Positive Working Relationships With Other Staff Members

Date: _____

When told private information about a student or staff person, demonstrate trustworthiness by keeping the information confidential. If you feel the person needs additional help, suggest a professional who specializes in the area of concern.

_____

_____

_____

Date: _____

Drop a note of appreciation into someone's mailbox today. Signing your name is optional. Building up an educator is a special gift.

_____

_____

_____

Date: _____

Listen with an open mind to the methods shared by others. Whether you use similar strategies or even disagree is irrelevant. Grant them the dignity of their professional judgment.

_____

_____

_____

Date: _____

Read professional articles presenting varied perspectives on education. Introduce your newfound information into a lounge conversation or staff meeting. Connect it with something that your faculty is doing well.

_____

_____

_____

Date: _____

Acknowledge extra efforts made by someone on your staff by a direct comment to him or her or through public praise in the lounge or at a staff meeting.

_____

_____

_____

Date: _____

Make it a habit to drop a note to anyone on staff who has been ill or experienced a recent personal loss.

_____

_____

_____

Date: _____

Notice a new or interesting article of clothing, tie, or jewelry worn by a coworker today. Be sure to mention it!

_____

_____

_____

Things to Do   *Goals*

_____ _____   _____ _____

_____ _____   _____ _____

_____ _____   _____ _____

_____ _____   _____ _____

_____ _____   _____ _____

_____ _____   _____ _____

October

ESTABLISHING POSITIVE WORKING RELATIONSHIPS WITH OTHER STAFF MEMBERS

Date: _____

When stopping by the cafeteria during lunchtime, comment on how the early hours and unique efforts of the food service staff contribute to the quality of your school lunch program.

_____

_____

_____

Date: _____

Honor the professional expertise of someone in a role different from yours. For example, ask the library clerk to recommend a suspenseful book you could read to your class.

_____

_____

_____

Date: _____

Bring a treat for the paraprofessional who helps you run off worksheets or supports children with special needs in your classroom.

_____

_____

_____

Date: _____

Accompany your students to their bus after school. Take a minute to affirm the drivers' daily efforts with their responsible and challenging job.

_____

_____

_____

Date: _____

Who on the staff appears somewhat tired, concerned, or overwhelmed today? What can you say or do to ease his or her burden?

_____

_____

_____

Date: _____

Take some time to learn the professional goals of one colleague. Offer him or her encouragement by expressing enthusiasm for his or her potential endeavors.

_____

_____

_____

Date: _____

Offer to bring popcorn to a beginning teacher's room after school. Share a funny story about your first year. Suggest creative ways to make his or her responsibilities more manageable.

_____

_____

_____

Things to Do   *Goals*

_____ _____   _____ _____

_____ _____   _____ _____

_____ _____   _____ _____

_____ _____   _____ _____

_____ _____   _____ _____

_____ _____   _____ _____

October–November

ESTABLISHING POSITIVE WORKING RELATIONSHIPS WITH OTHER STAFF MEMBERS

Date: _____

Leave a bouquet of flowers in the staff lounge sometime this week. Include a note addressed to "A Wonderful Bunch of Coworkers."

_____

_____

_____

Date: _____ New month!

Recognize the value of brief conversations with parents. Be fully present when you talk to them.

_____

_____

_____

Date: _____

Encourage parents to attend the open house by offering to take family pictures and provide copies of them.

_____

_____

_____

Date: _____

Write a classroom newsletter that features students with perfect attendance. Thank the parents for getting their children to school.

_____

_____

_____

ESTABLISHING A POSITIVE RAPPORT WITH PARENTS

Date: _____

Have small thank-you certificates ready. Each time a parent does something positive, send him or her one.

_____

_____

_____

Date: _____

At the end of each day, call at least one parent to relay something positive about his or her child.

_____

_____

_____

Date: _____

Give "Proud Parent" certificates to parents whose children have monthly perfect attendance, are showing extra effort, or have achieved good grades.

_____

_____

_____

Things to Do   *Goals*

_____ _____   _____ _____

_____ _____   _____ _____

_____ _____   _____ _____

_____ _____   _____ _____

_____ _____   _____ _____

_____ _____   _____ _____

ESTABLISHING A POSITIVE RAPPORT WITH PARENTS

Date: _____

Encourage parents to visit your classroom. Communicate that they are always welcome and suggest times for observing specific activities.

_____

_____

_____

Date: _____

Talk with your administrator about having a monthly "Coffee With the Teacher" meeting for parents. Develop discussion topics to guide the meetings.

_____

_____

_____

Date: _____

Send parents a list of recommended books or Web sites monthly.

_____

_____

_____

Date: _____

Order a stamp that says, "Good News From Mr./Ms. _____" or "Good News From School." You can stamp it on the outside of the envelope when you send a positive note home.

_____

_____

_____

Date: _____

Always start a parent conference with a positive statement. Discuss a child's strengths first.

_____

_____

_____

Date: _____

Provide parents with a list of things that they can do to help in the classroom. Include items that require a range of time commitments and projects that can be done at home.

_____

_____

_____

Date: _____

For families who have access to e-mail, periodically send an update on what's happening in your classroom. Print a copy of the message for students who do not have e-mail.

_____

_____

_____

Things to Do   *Goals*

_____ _____   _____ _____

_____ _____   _____ _____

_____ _____   _____ _____

_____ _____   _____ _____

_____ _____   _____ _____

_____ _____   _____ _____

ESTABLISHING A POSITIVE RAPPORT WITH PARENTS

Date: _____

If you have voice mail, record a cheery message each day. Outline any exciting events for that day and state the best time to reach you.

_____

_____

_____

Date: _____

Consider doing a one-page weekly newsletter. Use the newsletter to highlight positive events that occurred during the week.

_____

_____

_____

Date: _____

Have your students host an ice cream social or a tea to honor their parents.

_____

_____

_____

Date: _____

When you attend a meeting with a parent, sit next to him or her rather than across the table.

_____

_____

_____

Date: _____

Give homework assignments to students that encourage family time and are activity oriented, rather than solitary, paper-and-pencil activities.

_____

_____

_____

Date: _____

Ask parents for advice on what works best with their child.

_____

_____

_____

Date: _____

Ask parents to provide you with a brief history of the family—either written or oral—so that you can better understand the family culture.

_____

_____

_____

Things to Do   *Goals*

_____ _____   _____ _____

_____ _____   _____ _____

_____ _____   _____ _____

_____ _____   _____ _____

_____ _____   _____ _____

_____ _____   _____ _____

November

ESTABLISHING A POSITIVE RAPPORT WITH PARENTS

Date: _____

Ask the parents what their long-range goals are for their children.

_____

_____

_____

Date: _____

Have a classroom fun fair for families. Set up stations for activities that can be done in school or at home.

_____

_____

_____

Date: _____

Be a good listener. Often, parents just want someone to listen to the challenges they are facing. Advice may not be wanted or warranted.

_____

_____

_____

Date: _____

Involve parents in community service projects that your class is undertaking. Suggest ways that they can get involved and solicit ideas for future projects.

_____

_____

_____

Date: _____

   Give parents a preview of upcoming activities for your class. Give
them some concrete ideas on how they can help.

_____

_____

_____

Date: _____

   Prior to giving a lecture on a topic, send the parents your notes so that
they can discuss the topic with their child.

_____

_____

_____

Date: _____

   Periodically, send a little treat home to the parents with a note of
appreciation.

_____

_____

_____

Things to Do   *Goals*

_____ _____   _____ _____

_____ _____   _____ _____

_____ _____   _____ _____

_____ _____   _____ _____

_____ _____   _____ _____

_____ _____   _____ _____

November – December

ESTABLISHING A POSITIVE RAPPORT WITH PARENTS

Date: _____

Solicit from parents their most successful ideas for a given topic. For example, "How do you get your child to clean his room?" Compile the collection of ideas for all the parents.

_____

_____

_____

Date: _____

Host a cultural awareness fair for your classroom. Have each student work with his or her family to present a tradition from their culture. Invite parents to attend.

_____

_____

_____

Date: _____

Avoid using educator jargon. Some parents might not understand what you are saying and could be embarrassed to ask for clarification.

_____

_____

_____

Date: _____ New month!

Utilize "KWL" with students. **K** stands for what students **know**; **W** stands for what students **want** to learn; and **L** stands for what students **learned** after completing the lessons.

_____

_____

_____

SETTING STUDENTS UP FOR
ACADEMIC AND BEHAVIORAL SUCCESS

Date: _____

Incorporate students' names into worksheets and tests.

_____

_____

_____

Date: _____

If you assign more than one or two worksheets to students, let them choose the order in which they complete them.

_____

_____

_____

Date: _____

Keep students active in learning. Use shower curtains to create over-sized board games. Place the shower curtains on the floor and let the students use their own bodies as the game markers.

_____

_____

_____

Things to Do   *Goals*

_____ _____   _____ _____

_____ _____   _____ _____

_____ _____   _____ _____

_____ _____   _____ _____

_____ _____   _____ _____

_____ _____   _____ _____

December

SETTING STUDENTS UP FOR
ACADEMIC AND BEHAVIORAL SUCCESS

Date: _____

To work on matching words and definitions, make a large concentration board with 50 sections. Write the vocabulary words in 25 sections and the corresponding definitions in the remaining sections. Cover each section with a self-sticking note. Number the sections from 1 to 50 and challenge the students to a game of memory match.

_____

_____

_____

Date: _____

Have students individually graph their progress on skills that they want to improve.

_____

_____

_____

Date: _____

Give each student a blank Bingo card. When the student engages in a positive behavior, allow him or her to color in a square. When the student has colored all the squares, he or she earns a prize.

_____

_____

_____

Date: _____

Play "It's in the Bag." Cut strips of paper. Write a different assignment on each one. Put the strips in a bag and have each student draw one.

_____

_____

_____

Date: _____

Model positive self-talk for students. Encourage students to make positive comments before starting on a task, such as, "I know I can do this."

_____

_____

_____

Date: _____

Create a holiday tree display. Cut a class set of paper ornaments for the tree. Write an assignment on each one. Hang the ornaments on the tree, and let each student select one for his or her assignment.

_____

_____

_____

Date: _____

Give each student two craft sticks. Have the student write *yes* on one stick and *no* on the other. Ask a series of *yes/no* questions and let the students indicate their answers by holding up the appropriate stick.

_____

_____

_____

Things to Do   *Goals*

_____ _____   _____ _____

_____ _____   _____ _____

_____ _____   _____ _____

_____ _____   _____ _____

_____ _____   _____ _____

_____ _____   _____ _____

December

Setting Students Up for
Academic and Behavioral Success

Date: _____

Choose a topic you are learning about in class. Provide a list of statements about the topic. Include some true statements and some false statements. Have the students determine which are which.

_____

_____

_____

Date: _____

Have "Happy Gram" days. Give each student five blank Happy Grams. Then have each student draw names of five classmates. Encourage the students to write positive messages on the Happy Gram for each name drawn.

_____

_____

_____

Date: _____

Print handouts on different colors of paper.

_____

_____

_____

Date: _____

Integrate music throughout the day. Use calm music for creative assignments and marching music for transitions. Have students write their own songs to help them remember key points from assignments.

_____

_____

_____

Date: _____

Cut out question mark shapes and laminate them. Give each student a set of question marks. Have the students work together in study groups. Have each student ask members of his or her study group questions about a topic. For each question asked, the student relinquishes a question mark. Continue the study group until every student has relinquished all of his or her question marks.

_____

_____

_____

Date: _____

Use your students' real-life experiences whenever you can. For instance, if you are studying maps and directions, start with a map of the local community.

_____

_____

_____

Date: _____

If students tap their pencils, put a mouse pad on their desks to reduce the noise level.

_____

_____

_____

Things to Do   ***Goals***

_____ _____   _____ _____

_____ _____   _____ _____

_____ _____   _____ _____

_____ _____   _____ _____

_____ _____   _____ _____

_____ _____   _____ _____

December

SETTING STUDENTS UP FOR
ACADEMIC AND BEHAVIORAL SUCCESS

Date: _____

Establish a system for monitoring the amount of praise you use. Put pennies in one pocket, and each time you praise a student, move one penny to the other pocket. The goal is to move all of the pennies by the end of the day.

_____

_____

_____

Date: _____

Encourage students to praise one another. When you hear a student making a positive statement to another student, give him or her a special card to recognize those efforts.

_____

_____

_____

Date: _____

Introduce a task and model how you think aloud to approach the task. Practice together, and then have students do it on their own.

_____

_____

_____

Date: _____

Provide different colored visors for the students to wear during reading assignments. Periodically, stop the reading and have the students find a partner who is wearing a matching colored visor. For example, students wearing red visors are to find two concepts with which they agree and students wearing blue visors are to find two concepts with which they disagree.

_____

_____

_____

Date: _____

Teach children about graphic organizers. Show examples of graphic organizers, then let students experiment with what works best for them.

_____

_____

_____

Date: _____

Use your wardrobe as a way to enhance your lessons. For example, wear traditional clothing from countries that you are studying, or wear hats labeled with "Question Time" or "Quiet Time."

_____

_____

_____

Date: _____

This is the time of year to teach children the importance of giving to others. Do community service projects such as food drives or visiting a nursing home.

_____

_____

_____

Things to Do   *Goals*

_____ _____   _____ _____

_____ _____   _____ _____

_____ _____   _____ _____

_____ _____   _____ _____

_____ _____   _____ _____

_____ _____   _____ _____

SETTING STUDENTS UP FOR
ACADEMIC AND BEHAVIORAL SUCCESS

Date: _____

Show students how to take a complicated task and break it down into smaller steps. Work with the students to complete the steps, leaving the last one for them to do independently.

_____

_____

_____

Date: _____

Place pedals and foot massagers under the desks of students with ADHD so that they can move their feet without disrupting others.

_____

_____

_____

Date: _____

Let students use a set of numbered plastic balls to practice basic math facts.

_____

_____

_____

Date: _____

Let students use highlighters to organize written information. When using worksheets, have them highlight directions in yellow, vocabulary words in pink, and key points in purple.

_____

_____

_____

PREPARING STUDENTS FOR TEST TAKING

Date: _____

Use a "traveling notebook" to communicate with parents. Let the students carry the notebooks to and from school each day. Write notes to the parents in the notebooks and encourage them to write back to you.

_____

_____

_____

Date: _____

Write a positive note to each student. Be sure to compliment the student on something that he or she did during the past year and wish the student a happy New Year.

_____

_____

_____

Date: _____ New month!

Make a New Year's resolution to motivate your students to do well on state and local assessments. Plan lessons to teach them test-taking tips.

_____

_____

_____

Things to Do   *Goals*

_____ _____   _____ _____

_____ _____   _____ _____

_____ _____   _____ _____

_____ _____   _____ _____

_____ _____   _____ _____

_____ _____   _____ _____

PREPARING STUDENTS FOR TEST TAKING

Date: _____

Teach students a relaxation technique to utilize prior to taking a test. Have students close their eyes for 45 seconds while thinking of something that makes them happy.

_____

_____

_____

Date: _____

Teach students to highlight key direction words on practice tests.

_____

_____

_____

Date:_____

Have students practice taking timed tests. Give sample tests and have them graph their progress.

_____

_____

_____

Date: _____

Allow students to keep a cup or bottle of water on their desks during tests.

_____

_____

_____

Date: _____

Have each student make a test survival bag consisting of pencils, erasers, rulers, and whatever other tools they may need.

_____

_____

_____

Date: _____

Develop a proofreading checklist for students. Make a rubber stamp of the checklist and stamp it in the corner of tests given to students.

_____

_____

_____

Date: _____

Use practice tests with answer grids. Have students practice using the answer grids.

_____

_____

_____

Things to Do   *Goals*

January

Preparing Students for Test Taking

Date: _____

If students have trouble keeping their place on the answer grid, you may wish to enlarge the answer grid or the test questions.

_____

_____

_____

Date: _____

Some students may find it helpful to put their test on a clipboard. This will help to keep it from falling on the floor.

_____

_____

_____

Date: _____

If a student has high test anxiety on timed tests, have him or her sit away from other students who get the test done quickly.

_____

_____

_____

Date: _____

Teach students mnemonics to help them remember key facts. For example, HOMES can be used for remembering the names of the Great Lakes—Huron, Ontario, Michigan, Erie, and Superior.

_____

_____

_____

Date: _____

Rather than giving typical paper-and-pencil tests, give students a choice of either taking a written test or developing a game about the content learned.

_____

_____

_____

Date: _____

For each student, make a note regarding his or her test-taking skills in the file that will be passed on to next year's teacher. Such a note will help the new teacher gain additional insight about the student.

_____

_____

_____

Date: _____

Have students write vocabulary words on index cards and write the definitions on the opposite sides of the cards. Encourage the students to carry the cards with them to study.

_____

_____

_____

Things to Do   *Goals*

_____ _____   _____ _____

_____ _____   _____ _____

_____ _____   _____ _____

_____ _____   _____ _____

_____ _____   _____ _____

_____ _____   _____ _____

January

PREPARING STUDENTS FOR TEST TAKING

Date: _____

Determine whether special accommodations are needed for students taking tests. Think about how students receive the information and how they show what has been learned.

_____

_____

_____

Date: _____

Observe each student as he or she takes tests. Make notes on those observations and share them with educators who will administer future tests.

_____

_____

_____

Date: _____

Consider large-print materials for students with learning disabilities, with visual perception problems, or with emotional and behavioral problems.

_____

_____

_____

Date: _____

To teach note-taking skills, prepare a short lecture. Give the students an outline with a few blank spaces and have them complete the spaces. Increase the number of blank spaces each time you lecture.

_____

_____

_____

Date: _____

When grading tests, mark the number of correct responses rather than the number of wrong responses.

_____

_____

_____

Date: _____

Use clip art when designing tests to make them more interesting and to give necessary prompts.

_____

_____

_____

Date: _____

For students who are overwhelmed by seeing too much on a page, put a test sheet in a file folder. Cut the front cover of the file folder into four strips so that the student can flip over one strip at a time.

_____

_____

_____

Things to Do   *Goals*

_____   _____   _____   _____

_____   _____   _____   _____

_____   _____   _____   _____

_____   _____   _____   _____

_____   _____   _____   _____

PREPARING STUDENTS FOR TEST TAKING

Date: _____

When creating tests, avoid putting too much on one page. Leave as much white space as possible. For essay questions, leave plenty of room for the response.

_____

_____

_____

Date: _____

Teach children how to organize their key ideas before answering an essay question on a test.

_____

_____

_____

Date: _____

Prepare bookmarks for students that list helpful test-taking strategies.

_____

_____

_____

Date: _____

The day before a test, have each student submit a question about the material covered. Combine those questions into a test for the students.

_____

_____

_____

Date: _____

When possible, allow students to choose where they will sit while taking tests. Some students might prefer a study carrel, while others might prefer a table.

_____

_____

_____

Date: _____

When you are going to give a test, send notes home to parents. Ask them to set aside time for their children to study for the test.

_____

_____

_____

Date: _____

Set aside a few minutes before giving a test to allow students a bit of last minute studying.

_____

_____

_____

Things to Do   *Goals*

_____ _____   _____ _____

_____ _____   _____ _____

_____ _____   _____ _____

_____ _____   _____ _____

_____ _____   _____ _____

_____ _____   _____ _____

January – February

PREPARING STUDENTS FOR TEST TAKING

Date: _____

As a test review, have students write one key point on a self-sticking note, read the point to classmates, and post it on the board until test time.

_____

_____

_____

Date: _____

During testing, allow students to use headphones with soothing music. See if this decreases their anxiety and improves their test scores.

_____

_____

_____

Date: _____ New month!

Purchase rubber tubs to store your materials. Write a list of contents on the top and the sides of each tub so that when they are stacked, you can determine what is in each one.

_____

_____

_____

Date: _____

Purchase rubber tubs for students. Have the students keep their materials in the tubs, away from their desks. Allow them to only take materials out that are needed for each task.

_____

_____

_____

REFRESHING YOUR COLLECTION OF CLASSROOM ORGANIZATIONAL TIPS

Date: _____

Purchase a cardboard message center and label a slot for each student. Have the students put their completed assignments there. You can also use the message slots to deliver notes and other materials to the students.

_____

_____

_____

Date: _____

Before you file away a folder on a topic, go through it and save only what you absolutely need.

_____

_____

_____

Date: _____

Baskets are a great way to organize items on your desk or bookcase. Collect a variety of sizes for file folders, pens, and even business cards.

_____

_____

_____

Things to Do   *Goals*

_____ _____   _____ _____

_____ _____   _____ _____

_____ _____   _____ _____

_____ _____   _____ _____

_____ _____   _____ _____

_____ _____   _____ _____

REFRESHING YOUR COLLECTION OF CLASSROOM ORGANIZATIONAL TIPS

Date: _____

When you are required to complete forms containing information that does not change, complete that information on the blank form and photocopy the form with the information there.

_____

_____

_____

Date: _____

Keep a self-sticking note pad with you at all times, and write down tasks that need to be completed. When the task is done, throw the note away.

_____

_____

_____

Date: _____

Write down incident reports or logs by the end of each day. Otherwise, you start the next day behind and it is difficult to remember what actually happened.

_____

_____

_____

Date: _____

Carry a clipboard with you and write notes about what you need to do. At the end of the day, you can review your notes and prioritize your to-do list.

_____

_____

_____

Date: _____

Ask acquaintances who work in other fields to share with you their best organizational strategies. What can you adapt for your classroom?

_____

_____

_____

Date: _____

Each night, put the materials that you need for the following day by the front door at home, or put them in your car so they are not forgotten.

_____

_____

_____

Date: _____

If your mornings are rushed, do as much as possible to prepare in the evenings. For example, you may want to set the table for breakfast before going to bed.

_____

_____

_____

Things to Do   *Goals*

_____ _____   _____ _____

_____ _____   _____ _____

_____ _____   _____ _____

_____ _____   _____ _____

_____ _____   _____ _____

_____ _____   _____ _____

REFRESHING YOUR COLLECTION OF
CLASSROOM ORGANIZATIONAL TIPS

Date: _____

Label packets of forms needed for different types of meetings. When you have to attend a meeting, just pick up the packet of forms that you'll need.

_____

_____

_____

Date: _____

Always collect student work in the same place. It contributes to the students' sense of routine and eases your stress.

_____

_____

_____

Date: _____

Title a bulletin board "The 'In' Group." When a student turns in a project, place his or her picture on the bulletin board.

_____

_____

_____

Date: _____

List scheduled events on a large sheet of colored paper. Keep it posted for reference.

_____

_____

_____

Date: _____

Make desk cleaning a routine part of every week. As students become more aware of the location of their materials, they will save valuable class time.

_____

_____

_____

Date: _____

Spontaneously set a timer. Whenever it dings, ask, "Can you find your _____ (assignment, text, etc.)?" Students who show the item in 30 seconds earn a point toward a group reward.

_____

_____

_____

Date: _____

Help students keep track of the sequence of the day. Periodically, tell them what is coming next, how much time they have to complete a project, or how long it will be until lunchtime.

_____

_____

_____

Things to Do   *Goals*

_____ _____   _____ _____

_____ _____   _____ _____

_____ _____   _____ _____

_____ _____   _____ _____

_____ _____   _____ _____

_____ _____   _____ _____

REFRESHING YOUR COLLECTION OF
CLASSROOM ORGANIZATIONAL TIPS

Date: _____

When staying after school, meet your deadline for getting home by setting a timer. Leave when the timer goes off.

_____

_____

_____

Date: _____

Prioritize your daily duties and complete them with dedication.

_____

_____

_____

Date: _____

Develop a repertoire of ways to signal that you want your students' attention. Use a rhyme, a clapping pattern, or a chord cluster on the piano to get students to focus on your message.

_____

_____

_____

Date: _____

Determine the times of day when the majority of your coworkers work in their rooms or offices. When you need to do work requiring quiet concentration, plan to do it during a time when you are not likely to be interrupted.

_____

_____

_____

Date: _____

Be clear with coworkers when you are facing a deadline to complete a project. Ask for their understanding and arrange a time later for personal conversations.

_____

_____

_____

Date: _____

Take time at the beginning of each school year to anticipate busy periods, large workloads, and special deadlines. Plan your personal life accordingly so you are not too overloaded.

_____

_____

_____

Date: _____

Put all your attention on one task at a time. As you move from task to task, keep your attention focused.

_____

_____

_____

Things to Do   *Goals*

REFRESHING YOUR COLLECTION OF
CLASSROOM ORGANIZATIONAL TIPS

Date: _____

Place items to take to the office in a designated spot. Bring everything with you at once to avoid making extra trips down the hall.

_____

_____

_____

Date: _____

Arrange student seating for their best educational and behavioral advantage. Ask five students to create seating charts with the same objectives. Use the students' input in making the final decision.

_____

_____

_____

LEAP DAY!

Leap into this extra day with the determination to continuously clear out unnecessary papers, posters, or peripheral objects from your classroom.

_____

_____

_____

Date: _____   New month!

This month, consider having a spirit week with a special activity each day. You may want to include events such as dress up day, a silly socks day, and a favorite character costume day.

_____

_____

_____

MAINTAINING MOTIVATION, ENERGY, AND ENTHUSIASM FOR YOU AND YOUR STUDENTS

Date: _____

    Have a book theme week. Read a book appropriate to the age level of the students. Decorate your classroom like the setting in the book.

_____

_____

_____

Date: _____

    Teach your students a different exercise or flexibility stretch each day this month.

_____

_____

_____

Date: _____

    Adopt a special community service project this month. Possibilities include going to a nursing home, cleaning up the park, or assisting in a day care center.

_____

_____

_____

Things to Do   *Goals*

_____ _____   _____ _____

_____ _____   _____ _____

_____ _____   _____ _____

_____ _____   _____ _____

_____ _____   _____ _____

_____ _____   _____ _____

March

Maintaining Motivation, Energy, and Enthusiasm for You and Your Students

Date: _____

Teach a different stress reduction activity each day this month, such as blowing bubbles, deep breathing, and using a stress ball.

_____

_____

_____

Date: _____

Purchase a rubber ball and write stress reduction techniques on it. Toss the ball to each student, having them do the activity listed where their left thumb lands.

_____

_____

_____

Date: _____

Expose your students to various works of art this month.

_____

_____

_____

Date: _____

Have a "Beautify the Classroom" week. Invite the students to help beautify the room with plants, tablecloths, and other decorations.

_____

_____

_____

Date: _____

Make March a music appreciation month. Each day, expose the students to a different type of relaxation music. Have the students determine which types of music help them to learn, which types help them to relax, and which types help them to feel energized.

_____

_____

_____

Date: _____

Experiment with different air fresheners or hand lotions to find fragrances that are soothing. Be alert to students who have allergies.

_____

_____

_____

Date: _____

Have a Hobby Awareness month where students learn about different hobbies, such as stamp collecting. Invite students to create centers to teach each other about their hobbies.

_____

_____

_____

Things to Do   *Goals*

_____   _____   _____   _____

_____   _____   _____   _____

_____   _____   _____   _____

_____   _____   _____   _____

_____   _____   _____   _____

_____   _____   _____   _____

Maintaining Motivation, Energy, and Enthusiasm for You and Your Students

Date: _____

Take a self-improvement class and try to incorporate some of the strategies you learn in your classroom.

_____

_____

_____

Date: _____

Have students research their names and discover why they have the names they do. You can also expand this by having them create family trees.

_____

_____

_____

Date: _____

Students appreciate seeing photos of themselves. Take pictures and get each student his or her own photo album in which to place the photos. Encourage the students to write captions or stories to go with the pictures.

_____

_____

_____

Date: _____

Take a moment today to recall what motivated you to become a teacher.

_____

_____

_____

Date: _____

Depart from a detail in your lesson plans today and follow a creative impulse.

_____

_____

_____

Date: _____

Allow a student to take a break from routine and send an e-mail to his or her mom, dad, or guardians.

_____

_____

_____

Date: _____

Compliment a student today, taking notice of a small improvement that would ordinarily go unmentioned.

_____

_____

_____

Things to Do   *Goals*

_____ _____   _____ _____

_____ _____   _____ _____

_____ _____   _____ _____

_____ _____   _____ _____

_____ _____   _____ _____

Maintaining Motivation, Energy, and Enthusiasm for You and Your Students

Date: _____

Create an FYI Box. Set out slips of paper with the following prompts on them: "Teacher, I want to tell you _____." Near the bottom of the slips, have a place for the student to indicate whether or not a response from you is wanted.

_____

_____

_____

Date: _____

Create a "Composite Future" bulletin board. Have students bring in pictures of adults that they admire. Then have each student tell about the positive qualities represented by the photographs and how they can emulate those qualities.

_____

_____

_____

Date: _____

Spend some time watching the staff person you admire most. Consider how he or she keeps up his or her energy and professional motivation. How might you imitate his or her attitude and energetic actions?

_____

_____

_____

Date: _____

At the end of the day, mention to a student something about his or her work, behavior, or character that impressed you today.

_____

_____

_____

Date: _____

Select a student who is in need of encouragement or special attention to assist with an errand, demonstration, or dramatization of a concept.

_____

_____

_____

Date: _____

Consciously work to maintain a consistent attitude of appreciation toward a difficult student.

_____

_____

_____

Date: _____

Take time out today to read an article from a favorite professional journal, or read some passages from an educational book that has given you inspiration in the past.

_____

_____

_____

Things to Do   *Goals*

_____   _____   _____   _____

_____   _____   _____   _____

_____   _____   _____   _____

_____   _____   _____   _____

_____   _____   _____   _____

_____   _____   _____   _____

Maintaining Motivation, Energy, and Enthusiasm for You and Your Students

Date: _____

Visit another classroom to encourage the teacher about his or her efforts and successes. Then reflect on your own efforts and successes.

_____

_____

_____

Date: _____

Model your enthusiasm for learning as you present new concepts and ideas to students. Explain why an idea or concept interests and intrigues you.

_____

_____

_____

Date: _____

Recall the sights, sounds, and smells of your first day of school. Did anything influence or discourage your desire to learn? How can you use this information to affect your current class?

_____

_____

_____

Date: _____

Stop at a teacher supply shop or multipurpose store after school. Buy something you can use tomorrow to enhance the learning or social experience of your students.

_____

_____

_____

Renewing Your Spirit—Taking Care of You

Date: _____

Devise a strategy in the morning to complete the day on a positive note. Perhaps you could create a group goal or slogan to enhance tomorrow.

_____

_____

_____

Date: _____

Design a bulletin board or chart showing step-by-step student progress toward completing a behavioral or academic goal. Refer to this focal point daily until the end of the year.

_____

_____

_____

Date: _____ New month!

Shower yourself with praise and approval today. Note a professional success and give yourself credit for it.

_____

_____

_____

Things to Do   *Goals*

Renewing Your Spirit—Taking Care of You

Date: _____

Keep a notebook of all the challenges you've overcome as a teacher. Review it to strengthen your sense of competence and purpose.

_____

_____

_____

Date: _____

Add a healthy snack to the treats in the staff lounge by bringing in a vegetable or fruit plate. You'll have a choice besides the cake and cookies!

_____

_____

_____

Date: _____

Take time this evening to refresh yourself with a brisk walk in your neighborhood. Notice details in the homes, landscapes, and passing pedestrians.

_____

_____

_____

Date: _____

Put a favorite quote or inspirational picture on your desk. Review it frequently in order to gain the gift it gives you.

_____

_____

_____

Date: _____

Take time today to contact someone in your life who believes in your abilities and talents. Ask for his or her encouragement in your greatest current challenge.

_____

_____

_____

Date: _____

Find a quiet place in your school building where you can go when you need to regroup. Take some deep breaths and remind yourself of some of your positive traits.

_____

_____

_____

Date: _____

Sing a song from your childhood and appreciate the enthusiasm and energy it still provides you.

_____

_____

_____

Things to Do   *Goals*

_____ _____   _____ _____

_____ _____   _____ _____

_____ _____   _____ _____

_____ _____   _____ _____

_____ _____   _____ _____

_____ _____   _____ _____

RENEWING YOUR SPIRIT—TAKING CARE OF YOU

Date: _____

Offer to assist someone who appears to be stressed and tired. This not only benefits him or her, but also helps distract you from your own work-related concerns.

_____

_____

_____

Date: _____

Look out a window and focus on the sky. Note passing cloud patterns, weather conditions, and seasonal signals in plants.

_____

_____

_____

Date: _____

Plan a mini-break after school. Pick up a favorite magazine and a snack food. Enjoy a little time to yourself before going home.

_____

_____

_____

Date: _____

Keep "crunchy munchies" in your desk drawer for quick energy. Release stress and anger with the snap of peanut shells, or snack on popcorn to help you slow down your pace.

_____

_____

_____

Date: _____

   When your workload overwhelms you, step out into the hall and take a drink of water from a nearby fountain.

_____

_____

_____

Date: _____

   Be open to your own thoughts and attitudes that lead to maximizing self-care and more balanced living. Follow through on these possibilities.

_____

_____

_____

Date: _____

   Whenever you feel tired or discouraged, reroute your energies and attitudes with a flexibility stretch. Follow this with an affirmation asserting your teaching talents.

_____

_____

_____

Things to Do   *Goals*

Renewing Your Spirit—Taking Care of You

Date: _____

After school, take off your shoes, wiggle your toes, and giggle. Things can get pretty serious in this business!

_____

_____

_____

Date: _____

Schedule time for yourself, whether it is to take a hot bath or to go on a weekend retreat. Enjoy the benefits of inner inspiration and quiet.

_____

_____

_____

Date: _____

Fantasize about a future vacation and look forward to taking this time for fun and refreshment. Feel free to release professional pressures and thoughts of school.

_____

_____

_____

Date: _____

Imagine the benefits of a healthy diet, consistent exercise program, and a good night's sleep. Envision their impact on your job performance and take steps to bring it about.

_____

_____

_____

Date: _____

Pamper yourself. Make an appointment for an after school massage or manicure.

_____

_____

_____

Date: _____

Reserve tickets for a play or concert that interests you. Maybe a coworker would like to attend with you.

_____

_____

_____

Date: _____

Do something crafty and creative tonight. Try painting, woodcarving, knitting, or writing. Do whatever calms your mind and revives your spirit.

_____

_____

_____

Things to Do   *Goals*

RENEWING YOUR SPIRIT—TAKING CARE OF YOU

Date: _____

Visit your local library on the way home from school. Check out a book about a subject entirely unrelated to your teaching position and discover a new interest.

_____

_____

_____

Date: _____

Take a nap for ten minutes before dinner. Just let the school day go and relax. Plan to resume your duties at home with more focus and energy.

_____

_____

_____

Date: _____

Bring a novel or magazine to school. Opt to eat lunch alone while enjoying a brief diversion from school's daily demands.

_____

_____

_____

Date: _____

Disappear into a crowded mall for anonymity in order to experience some contrast to your public role as teacher.

_____

_____

_____

Date: _____

Before going home, stop at a nature center. Breathe in the fresh air and soak in the late afternoon sunshine.

_____

_____

_____

Date: _____

Rent a book on tape and enjoy a mystery or adventure story in the car while driving to and from school.

_____

_____

_____

Date: _____

Cultivate your spirituality according to your own beliefs and practices. Reflect on ways this supports and enriches your teaching experience.

_____

_____

_____

Things to Do   *Goals*

_____ _____   _____ _____

_____ _____   _____ _____

_____ _____   _____ _____

_____ _____   _____ _____

_____ _____   _____ _____

_____ _____   _____ _____

REVIEWING YOUR LEGACY TO STUDENTS, FAMILY, AND STAFF

Date: _____

Purchase a bouquet of fresh flowers or a small budding plant for your desk. Enjoy!

_____

_____

_____

Date: _____ New month!

Take time this month to remember the most powerful and profound moment of this past school year. Where were you? Review the details of the experience.

_____

_____

_____

Date: _____

Now that the year is winding down, is there something you would like to tell your class about yourself that you still have not said?

_____

_____

_____

Date: _____

Consider ways you've inspired coworkers during this school year. Was it by sharing material or by modeling a teaching technique or an attitude?

_____

_____

_____

Date: _____

Recall the first day of the current teaching term. What were your hopes, dreams, and plans for your students? Did things play out as you had planned?

_____

_____

_____

Date: _____

Has this year gone by quickly or did it seem endless? Does your sense of time indicate anything about your assessment of the success of this year?

_____

_____

_____

Date: _____

Think through your curricular areas and consider what deepened your understanding of the material and enhanced your presentation skills.

_____

_____

_____

Things to Do   *Goals*

_____ _____   _____ _____

_____ _____   _____ _____

_____ _____   _____ _____

_____ _____   _____ _____

_____ _____   _____ _____

_____ _____   _____ _____

Reviewing Your Legacy to Students, Family, and Staff

Date: _____

Ask yourself how being in the company of this year's students made you more mature. Are you more tolerant of their developmental abilities? Are you more sensitive to their personal issues?

_____

_____

_____

Date: _____

Recall something that greatly impacted your entire staff—a unique challenge or success that someone at your school experienced, a collective issue faced by all the educators in your district, or even a national event that inspired people to act. Has this occurrence changed you?

_____

_____

_____

Date: _____

Reflect on ways that you've encouraged your students to respect the environment. Would something you modeled motivate them to treat the Earth with more tenderness and care?

_____

_____

_____

Date: _____

Review your interactions with students, whether formal or informal, as if you were a third party. Realize that your presence has been a unique, unrepeatable gift in their lives.

_____

_____

_____

Date: _____

Note your personal habits throughout the day. Do you notice any students who imitate your style of communication or your phrases and mannerisms?

_____

_____

_____

Date: _____

Students don't always verbalize their appreciation. If they put their sentiments into words, how would they express their gratitude? Write yourself a note or letter emblematic of student appreciation.

_____

_____

_____

Date: _____

Before or after school, walk the halls. Note the decorations and people you see. Internally respond to them with acknowledgment of their contribution to your life as an educator.

_____

_____

_____

Things to Do   *Goals*

_____ _____   _____ _____

_____ _____   _____ _____

_____ _____   _____ _____

_____ _____   _____ _____

_____ _____   _____ _____

REVIEWING YOUR LEGACY TO STUDENTS, FAMILY, AND STAFF

Date: _____

Acknowledge a parent's efforts to assist his or her child with a challenge the child overcame during the school year.

_____

_____

_____

Date: _____

Map out the course of your relationship with selected parents. Note the trust level as it began and developed, your offers of support, and the relationship's growth.

_____

_____

_____

Date: _____

Examine the atmosphere of your room, your work team, and your building and recognize your positive impact on them.

_____

_____

_____

Date: _____

When you drive out of the parking lot tonight, think self-affirming thoughts. Recognize yourself for your gestures of respect and acts of kindness toward students and staff.

_____

_____

_____

Date: _____

Take a moment to be grateful for your coworkers; accept their talents, personalities, and even their flaws. Consider the privilege it's been to work in their presence each day.

_____

_____

_____

Date: _____

Ask yourself what your students, parents, and coworkers would have lost if you had not been present during this past year.

_____

_____

_____

Date: _____

Shake the hand of a student, staff member, or parent today. Make this tactile contact a symbolic expression of why you are here: to better the lives of others.

_____

_____

_____

Things to Do   *Goals*

_____ _____   _____ _____

_____ _____   _____ _____

_____ _____   _____ _____

_____ _____   _____ _____

_____ _____   _____ _____

_____ _____   _____ _____

REVIEWING YOUR LEGACY TO STUDENTS, FAMILY, AND STAFF

Date: _____

View your day through the eyes of an educator from 100 years ago. What might this person think is absolutely "awesome" about your teaching style and situation?

_____

_____

_____

Date: _____

Do you remember the funniest thing that happened all year? Remind your students today of the good laugh you had on that occasion.

_____

_____

_____

Date: _____

Envision meeting your most successful and most challenging student 20 years from today. How would each of you complete the following? "Because of you, I thankfully say I am now _____."

_____

_____

_____

Date: _____

Think back to a time of conflict you experienced with a student, staff person, or parent. Take a step today to reroute that relationship to a more positive direction.

_____

_____

_____

Date: _____

When you experienced anger, discouragement, or frustration in the presence of others, how did you model appropriate expression of emotion? Commend yourself for teaching valuable life lessons to them.

_____

_____

_____

Date: _____

Plan to celebrate the last day by writing an end of the year song, writing a clever riddle about each child, or taking a comical class picture. Imagine the surprise!

_____

_____

_____

Date: _____

Imagine yourself as an invisible guest at the dinner table of each student's family. Listen to them tell their family members why this was their favorite school year yet.

_____

_____

_____

Things to Do   *Goals*

_____ _____   _____ _____

_____ _____   _____ _____

_____ _____   _____ _____

_____ _____   _____ _____

_____ _____   _____ _____

_____ _____   _____ _____

REVIEWING YOUR LEGACY TO STUDENTS, FAMILY, AND STAFF

Date: _____

Complete for each student or selected class: "You're excellent at _____. Keep it up in the future!" Present it in a sealed envelope as they leave on the last day.

_____

_____

_____

Date: _____

Partner with a peer who knows you very well. Give one another an end-of-the-year "positive peppering." Share your observations of one another's strengths and successes.

_____

_____

_____

Date: _____

Write about a moment of grace when everything lined up and your teaching soul glistened. Save it for personal support on a future day when you definitely need it.

_____

_____

_____

Date: _____

Pause at exactly 10:17 A.M. today and take a few seconds to savor the sights, sounds, smells, and sense of satisfaction in being a teacher.

_____

_____

_____

ENRICHING YOUR PERSONAL AND FAMILY LIFE

Date: _____

Look at the life of a relative, either living or deceased, who works (or worked) as an educator. What makes (or made) this teacher tick?

_____

_____

_____

Date: _____

Create a talent tree. Sketch the outline of a tree and on each branch write the name of a gift or a skill that you possess or are developing. Notice how these abilities and talents enrich you.

_____

_____

_____

Date: _____

Schedule time to get together with a long-time friend you've not seen lately because of school demands.

_____

_____

_____

Things to Do   *Goals*

Enriching Your Personal and Family Life

Date: _____

Plan an out-of-town trip to visit a relative. Renew memories and catch up on life events that have occurred this past school year.

_____

_____

_____

Date: _____

With the summer season, there is more time to stay home. Pause to talk to a neighbor and take an interest in the latest news in his or her life.

_____

_____

_____

Date: _____

Who in your immediate family have you missed the most due to job-related commitments? Set up special time with that person for the day after school officially ends.

_____

_____

_____

Date: _____

Take time to address issues left unattended during the school year. Perhaps a talk with a relative, friend, clergyperson, or therapist would help you to move forward.

_____

_____

_____

Date: _____

Challenge your family members or friends to select one athletic activity to monitor for improvement. Hold one another accountable for achieving the selected goals.

_____

_____

_____

Date: _____

Organize a surprise potluck dinner. Write different courses of a meal on pieces of paper and have each guest draw the course that he or she will provide for the potluck.

_____

_____

_____

Date: _____

Write the names of people that you have not seen in a while on slips of paper. Draw a name each Sunday. Call or e-mail that person during the week.

_____

_____

_____

Things to Do   *Goals*

_____ _____   _____ _____

_____ _____   _____ _____

_____ _____   _____ _____

_____ _____   _____ _____

_____ _____   _____ _____

_____ _____   _____ _____

ENRICHING YOUR PERSONAL AND FAMILY LIFE

Date: _____

In a notebook, create headers as follows: Videos/DVDS, Books, Comments. Keep a running record of your reading and video viewing.

_____

_____

_____

Date: _____

Designate a quiet space in your home or yard. Retreat there when you need a few moments of peace. Even a backyard bench by a birdbath will do.

_____

_____

_____

Date: _____

Invite a few coworkers over for lunch. Plan to keep school out of the conversation as much as possible.

_____

_____

_____

Date: _____

Remember the things you did during the summer when you were a child. Choose one of these activities and go play!

_____

_____

_____

Date: _____

Clear away clutter from your living space one room at a time. (This could include your classroom.) Plan a garage sale, or give excess items to a charitable organization.

_____

_____

_____

Date: _____

Make a holiday shopping list and begin your gift buying early. Find treasures at sidewalk sales and on your travels that will delight your friends and relatives in December.

_____

_____

_____

Date: _____

Think of a hobby or a talent in which you have reached a plateau of skill. Sign up for lessons and advance to another level.

_____

_____

_____

Things to Do   *Goals*

_____ _____   _____ _____

_____ _____   _____ _____

_____ _____   _____ _____

_____ _____   _____ _____

_____ _____   _____ _____

_____ _____   _____ _____

ENRICHING YOUR PERSONAL AND FAMILY LIFE

Date: _____

Plan an intergenerational party with family and friends. Do some cross-generational partnering during party activities.

_____

_____

_____

Date: _____

Observe employees in any nonschool site. Imagine yourself working there and compare this work environment with your school. List the advantages of teaching and read this list in September.

_____

_____

_____

Date: _____

Bring out photographs from a past vacation or event. Connect with family or friends to share memories and special thoughts about the occasion.

_____

_____

_____

Date: _____

Make a date with yourself to wind down from the school year. While sitting on a beach watching sailboats or resting in a hammock, let go of classroom memories.

_____

_____

_____

Date: _____

Choose a value that you consider a priority for your life. Invite family or friends to discuss famous or familiar people who model this trait. Consider ways to emulate these people.

_____

_____

_____

Date: _____

Look in your community newspaper for listings of free concerts, speakers, or special events. Make an effort to attend at least one.

_____

_____

_____

Date: _____

Venture into another area of town. Have lunch, window shop, read ads on telephone poles, people watch, or strike up a conversation with someone in a coffee shop.

_____

_____

_____

Things to Do   *Goals*

_____ _____   _____ _____

_____ _____   _____ _____

_____ _____   _____ _____

_____ _____   _____ _____

_____ _____   _____ _____

_____ _____   _____ _____

ENRICHING YOUR PERSONAL AND FAMILY LIFE

Date: _____

Bring your teaching talents to a nearby nursing home. Listen to a resident's stories about his or her childhood, lead a craft project, or share some other talent with the residents.

_____

_____

_____

Date: _____

Explore your political opinions and personal perspectives as news events unfold. Learn in-depth information about the topic. Read magazines or watch news analysis programs.

_____

_____

_____

Date: _____

Befriend an immigrant new to your community. Learn about his or her background and reasons for coming to this country. Consider inviting this person to give a presentation in your classroom when school resumes.

_____

_____

_____

Date: _____

Enjoy summer as it unfolds. Put school on the back burner. Move out of your teacher identity, stepping further into your role as a parent, a friend, a citizen, and so on.

_____

_____

_____

June – July

Benefiting From Professional Development

Date: _____

Get up early to enjoy the sounds, sights, and smells of morning. Relax and start the day knowing that you won't be required to rush off to school. Instead, read something inspirational.

_____
_____
_____

Date: _____

What would you enjoy doing the most before school starts? Make sure you make time to do it before summer is over!

_____
_____
_____

Date: _____ New month!

Remember, professional development can be accomplished by different methods. Think of ways you can learn about your profession—searching the Internet, reading professional journals, taking workshops and classes, and so on.

_____
_____
_____

Things to Do   *Goals*

_____ _____   _____ _____
_____ _____   _____ _____
_____ _____   _____ _____
_____ _____   _____ _____
_____ _____   _____ _____
_____ _____   _____ _____

July

BENEFITING FROM PROFESSIONAL DEVELOPMENT

Date: _____

Join professional organizations. You will gain access to journals, Web sites, conferences, and new friends.

_____

_____

_____

Date: _____

Attend professional organizations' conventions. Not only will you learn about the latest hot topics, but you will also have a wonderful opportunity to meet people with similar interests and concerns.

_____

_____

_____

Date: _____

Join a Listserv of individuals interested in a topic that interests you.

_____

_____

_____

Date: _____

Sign up for e-mail newsletters to receive the latest information on educational topics.

_____

_____

_____

Date: _____

Prior to attending an inservice, do a search on the Internet for background information on the topic.

_____

_____

_____

Date: _____

While there is work involved in being a board member of an organization, the benefits you reap far outweigh the work. You grow professionally and establish long-lasting relationships. Consider getting involved in an organization that you belong to.

_____

_____

_____

Date: _____

To revive yourself, join organizations that relate to your intellectual interests and hobbies.

_____

_____

_____

Things to Do   *Goals*

_____ _____   _____ _____

_____ _____   _____ _____

_____ _____   _____ _____

_____ _____   _____ _____

_____ _____   _____ _____

_____ _____   _____ _____

BENEFITING FROM PROFESSIONAL DEVELOPMENT

Date: _____

Get involved in community organizations to broaden your horizons. You will gain valuable insight into community members' perspectives outside of education.

_____

_____

_____

Date: _____

Consider starting an early morning book club. Get together once a month with members to discuss a recently released book.

_____

_____

_____

Date: _____

When you receive your educational journals, skim through them for articles that interest you. Read and share with others. Cut the articles out and file them by topic.

_____

_____

_____

Date: _____

When you go to conferences you can't attend every session, but many conferences sell session audio tapes. Buy some to listen to in the car during your work commute.

_____

_____

_____

Date: _____

　Use your experiences during inservice workshops to reflect on how your students feel sitting in class. What motivating techniques is the speaker using to maintain interest?

_____

_____

_____

Date: _____

　When attending conferences, visit exhibits at closing time and ask for free samples of classroom materials. Exhibitors may give away materials that they don't want to pack and take back with them.

_____

_____

_____

Date: _____

　Share information that you gained from attending a conference and encourage others to do the same.

_____

_____

_____

Things to Do   *Goals*

_____ _____   _____ _____

_____ _____   _____ _____

_____ _____   _____ _____

_____ _____   _____ _____

_____ _____   _____ _____

_____ _____   _____ _____

BENEFITING FROM PROFESSIONAL DEVELOPMENT

Date: _____

All educators must be lifelong learners. Seize opportunities to attend workshops and conferences.

_____

_____

_____

Date: _____

Plan one follow-up activity as a result of attending a conference—read a book or an article, or learn more about a technique.

_____

_____

_____

Date: _____

If you attend a conference session and find it is not appropriate, discreetly leave and attend another session.

_____

_____

_____

Date: _____

If you wish to attend what might be a popular session at a conference, be sure to arrive early to get a seat.

_____

_____

_____

Date: _____

Mentoring programs are good for all parties. If you are experienced, mentor a new teacher. If you are a new teacher, seek out an experienced teacher to learn from.

_____

_____

_____

Date: _____

Get together with another teacher and observe in each other's classrooms. This will help you to gain new ideas and strategies and to learn about different teaching styles.

_____

_____

_____

Date: _____

Sign up for a class on a topic of personal interest, such as exercise, photography, or writing.

_____

_____

_____

Things to Do   *Goals*

_____   _____   _____   _____

_____   _____   _____   _____

_____   _____   _____   _____

_____   _____   _____   _____

_____   _____   _____   _____

_____   _____   _____   _____

BENEFITING FROM PROFESSIONAL DEVELOPMENT

Date: _____

   Adopt a positive attitude about faculty meetings. Instead of complaining about another meeting, be happy that you are part of the process and provide productive input.

_____

_____

_____

Date: _____

   When attending a staff development session, take a professional book or article with you. You may have a few minutes here and there in which you can read a few pages.

_____

_____

_____

Date: _____

   Take business cards with you to conferences. Exchange cards with people with whom you want to network.

_____

_____

_____

Date: _____

   Volunteer to speak at a conference. Have confidence in your ability to speak and share techniques that work in your classroom. Educators want to hear from working practitioners.

_____

_____

_____

Date: _____

When attending a conference, enjoy the after-session hours by going to dinner or on fun-filled excursions with other attendees.

_____

_____

_____

Date: _____

Professional development is a lifelong process. There is so much to learn from a variety of sources. Never stop seizing the opportunities that await you.

_____

_____

_____

Date: _____

Check to see whether your district will pay for your membership in a professional organization, and take advantage of that opportunity.

_____

_____

_____

Things to Do   *Goals*

_____ _____   _____ _____

_____ _____   _____ _____

_____ _____   _____ _____

_____ _____   _____ _____

_____ _____   _____ _____

_____ _____   _____ _____

Benefiting From Professional Development

Date: _____

While at a conference, attend poster sessions or table talk sessions. These are great ways to pick up a lot of information in a short time.

_____

_____

_____

Date: _____

This journal is a great professional development tool. Periodically look back on your reflections and use that information to improve your everyday life.

_____

_____

_____

Things to Do   *Goals*

_____ _____   _____ _____

_____ _____   _____ _____

_____ _____   _____ _____

_____ _____   _____ _____

_____ _____   _____ _____

_____ _____   _____ _____

**CORWIN
PRESS**

The Corwin Press logo—a raven striding across an open book—represents the union of courage and learning. Corwin Press is committed to improving education for all learners by publishing books and other professional development resources for those serving the field of PreK–12 education. By providing practical, hands-on materials, Corwin Press continues to carry out the promise of its motto: **"Helping Educators Do Their Work Better."**